EMOTIONAL SUPPORT HORSE

Claudine Toutoungi is a poet and playwright. She was born in Warwickshire, studied English and French at Trinity College, Oxford and has worked as an actor, a BBC radio drama producer, an English teacher, and a Royal Literary Fund Writing Fellow for Newnham and Selwyn Colleges in Cambridge. Carcanet published her debut poetry collection *Smoothie* in 2017. This was followed by *Two Tongues* (2020), which won the Ledbury Munthe Poetry Prize for Second Collections. Her poetry has been translated into Spanish and her live poetry contributions to festivals include Tongue Fu, Poetry East and appearances on BBC Radio 4. Her plays for theatre include *Bit Part* and *Slipping* (Stephen Joseph Theatre), and her many audio dramas for BBC Radio 4 include *Deliverers*, *The Inheritors* and *The Voice in my Ear*. She lives in Cambridge.

T0349371

Emotional
Support
Horse
Claudine
Toutoungi

CARCANET POETRY

First published in Great Britain in 2024 by
Carcanet
Alliance House, 30 Cross Street
Manchester, M 2 7 A Q
www.carcanet.co.uk

ISBN 978 1 80017 447 4

Cover design by Neilson MacKay
Book design by Andrew Latimer, Carcanet
Typesetting by LiteBook Prepress Services
Printed in Great Britain by SRP Ltd, Exeter, Devon

The publisher acknowledges financial
assistance from Arts Council England.

CONTENTS

EMOTIONAL SUPPORT HORSE

SHORTEST DAY

Recently a woman told a group of people they should be prepared
because I am the kind of person likely to get close up to your face.

The sky is losing light very fast like a patient bleeding out on a table.
I perform a series of regular movements listening to the wind.

The wind has a lot to say. It is long-winded. Old roué. Old reprobate.
Never knowingly not taking its valedictory lap around the garden.

It used to be infinitely sad in this empty kitchen and the skittering
of the leaves at its edges would have driven me out beyond the brink

but it's ok now. The radiator's on and outside has cornered the market
in confusion. When I came back from my short walk earlier

you asked was the post box full like you were worried those letters
wouldn't fit. The wind is having a laugh. *Ha ha ho* it goes

like a dead judge back from the grave for one final filibuster.
I have never knowingly got up close to anyone I don't know's face.

*

LAZARUS

The little fly you squashed and put into the ashtray
—how it walked out later that same day, bold as
you like across the carpet, cold-shouldering your

botched attempt at homicide with the aloofness of a
hired gun to the extent you broke into guffaws then
fell, stricken, to your knees and sobbed, forgiving

every one of your murderous intentions, forgiving
yourself, letting the patch of sun claim its prize.

MAPLES

we have them on all sides surrounded
we make eyes at yellows and reds
we crumble bits and inhale maple dust

one woman walks by with a dog in a pram
the dog husks Montand's nostalgic
classic *Les Feuilles Mortes*

and three old men nod
they have been ceremoniously buried
up to their chins in spiky little leaves

but make no fuss
puffing on pipes they cannot remove
bald heads blessed with twigs and detritus

CONVERSATION IN LEAMINGTON

I had breakfast with father
four weeks into the first stage
of grief. We discussed politics,
pork medallions. I told him his
choisya was in full bloom.
Later I took to my bed
for the usual three-hour lull.
I regretted the mass of
quandaries I could have
touched on but shelved.
For what? For why? I could
have cried out—father, where
am I now, with you gone? I've
crossed the Rubicon but I don't
have a map and that bird you liked,
the little one, it's always off-kilter,
always in a flap, with a coloratura
that pays no heed to the basics
of pitch and melody and daily since
you went I narrate everything I do.
And I walk on my hands a lot,
in the garden, like a crab—and the lists,
my God, father, the lists I keep: flower names,
trees, female mystics, the villages
of Warwickshire and one that
grows longer as we speak:
burnt tongue, slapped cheek,
railway spine... all the arcane ailments
I swear I've got. Yesterday I saw two horses
on Blue Cedar Grove. Two—on a road
never normally troubled by anything

larger than a wolfhound, but why tell you that?
Why recount and recount as if in the grip of
emergency... the visit to the windmill, the stray
lupin, the fact there's a village called Wormleighton
—where does it stop? Could I tell you so much
I'd narrate myself out of existence—return, like you,
to a purer state? Beyond exposition. No need
of that. Somewhere between an oscillation
and laughter.

was no longer there when we got to the brow of the hill
and St Lawrence's churchyard. Try as we might, we could
find no historic plaque explaining the ways in which demons
vacated the nave on important occasions. We hoped it was

orderly and lingered awhile, deciphering headstones, only
running into a septuagenarian who came here often, he told
us, to look for a girlfriend he'd had, but had lost. Fresh
flowers on the plot where her parents were stowed and he

took heart from that (his wife in the car, the engine idling).
If he came back enough, he said, he felt sure he'd find her.
A curious spot. Where others had sat to watch the bombs
drop on Coventry. We shivered. Baa-ed at a sheep. Moved on.

THE BIRDS

the birds have got their eye on you
they peep regularly

previously you were close
but then you and the birds drifted

the birds do not believe in full disclosure
they are playing the kazoo

they know you have a thing
about their wings

the birds are not up for grabs
they don't give a toss about your eco-gazebo

ditto your vegan-friendly bird feeder
the birds are not vegans

and not particularly friendly
their grace notes teem with conjecture

the birds and your scarified lawn
the birds and the thousand natural shocks

the birds yell all day in the arbour
heaven forfend! they yell

beshrew my heart!
iconoclasts of the rockery

goliaths of the thicket
you do not have the luxury of chaos

but the birds do and the birds
are making free with it

THE PARTY

In the midst of life I told my host (who was in the kitchen) I needed
to slip out and stagger about in the yard for a bit and potentially
regurgitate into a woodpile the nibbles I'd hoovered up after a 4hr
jamming session, during which I'd played bongos beatifically then
got locked in the toilet for hours because everyone else was busy
making jazz hands and scatting and they thought the screaming
was part of the music and the music worked well with my screams

DON'T WORRY ABOUT ME—

I'm ok, I have reached the higher echelons.

They have dispensed with midges in the higher
echelons and the air is sweet with marjoram and mint.

We are awash with flowers, the little ones, called
everlastings, and the nettles in the nettle patch contain

no capacity to sting. Don't worry about me

—there is miniature golf, skinny-dipping (practically
de rigueur) and Verdi by the lake, where highland cows

confront us. Beautiful, though I give them a wide berth.

DETOUR

Strange to come upon them shoving and rubbing
shoulders (without shoulders), charging about

a sure-fire shoal, a mass of marmalade bodies
in perpetual, Brownian motion. Why should I feel

so buoyed up by them? Or that I did right to spurn
the Cast Iron plant, skirt the Yucca and, glancing

down, spy them? I have seen the signs. I have
heard the spheres dancing. O celestial slipstream!

O quixotic drift of all that is dart and dazzle. I have lost
my mind! I have left it in a fountain in Birmingham.

and stare perplexedly into the middle distance
with one crease, one particularly characterful
furrow knitting my brow, not an old lady furrow
oh no something about the way I hold this furrow
in this ongoingly perplexed stare will imply a whole
panoply of barely suppressed emotions, a gamut
even, simmering away under the surface of this
singular furrow topped off with an immensely
enigmatic rage that also, paradoxically, resembles
rapture and I will do banter in my cop car with my
sidekick oh definitely I want a sidekick with whom
I will stop. Unwontedly. Here. And also sometimes
there. And I will chew my lip. And he will hold his
breath. Bamboozled by my odd. Choice. Of hiatus.
And no one will move until I speak again.

A CONSULTATION

You need to do more formalised walking the doctor said.
Why not buy one of those formalised walking devices
that measures your tread? They're good. I had one and
loved it until I felt it was judging me. Then I stamped on it.

I liked this doctor—Lebrun was his name. To some degree
he was nondescript but now and again he would flare up
with a blazing, fellow warmth. It made him hard to contradict.
Or skipping, he added, placing one hand on my shoulder—

if formalised walking gets you down, why not skip? Many
believe jumping daily, with or without a rope, staves off
melancholy. And keep a skipping journal but don't write
down anything about how much you skip or how long it

took or how fast your heart was beating after. Scrap all that.
What it was I should write was my next enquiry, made with a
childish tremor in my voice that I wished fervently to subdue.
I am not a scholarly man said Lebrun, *but perhaps this—*

and he handed me a calfskin notebook—the pages mostly
blank but for two at the centre, where over and over until
I was dizzy I read, in his looping hand: *Motion is emotion*
is motion is emotion is motion is emotion is motion.

AT SEZINCOTE

three brass serpents bared their fangs and the
hush-hush-hush of the flaming canopy, fallen
beneath our feet, shushed our debate as to

the etymology of the house's name and what
exactly we might hope to find within the Thornery
as opposed to the Lower Thornery, until, at last,

all queried-out, we came upon an ornamental
lake into which the willow and the hornbeam
were doing our weeping for us, so off we went,

up a slope, and at the top felt again the
jolt of your incontrovertible absence—like
closeness. Like really you were here.

MISSTEP

I always like a bare-branched tree in winter.
The branches remind me of my dendrites.
Likewise a swoop of unidentified dive-
bombers can be companionable when there's
frost to crunch and elsewhere only the odd,
demented cackle from a fly-by, loner crow.
And my shadow's out in front, like I've a friend
leading the way. *Je suis à la file indienne
avec mon ombre*, you might say, if you were
trying to impress an intellectual, the sort who
later, over speciality hummus, might delicately
bring up your choice of old world diction and
raise an eyebrow at it, musing on locutions
that, really, didn't ought to be.

WE COULDN'T GET THE PARTS TO WRITE THIS POEM

Our metaphor container ship is dry-docked
in Bratislava and our simile warehouse in
Wuppertal has had to close its doors.

We apologise. Some figments, we believe,
may still be in transit, but there are supply chain
fractures due to disputes over paperwork.

We're so sorry that we couldn't get the parts
but the task has not been helped by a general
dip in the market for lyricism in the West

and in the East by surveillance tactics to curb
outbreaks of oxymorons, iambics, and random
enjambment. The rise in divorce rates between

couplets has also been unprecedented and many
of the major manufacturers of pathetic fallacy
have changed profession, citing burnout.

We did try to let some fancies flee away
but they got caught up in the jet blast
of a cargo plane over the South China Sea.

They went from a/b/a/b to *Mayday, Mayday*
and, sadly, nosedived. Once again, we apologise.
We'll post here if normal service can resume.

WHEN I WALKED INTO THE WATER WEARING RED SHOES IN DECEMBER

I was desperate for a metaphor
it was a *cri de coeur*
I subliminally hoped to climb back into the womb
or collapse the perpendicular
or rub shoulders with the heron
I was devolving navigation from my eyes to my skin
or my shadow-self called
or my process unravelled
I was being swirled insistently in the river's comradely grip
it was protest poetry
I was reappraising gravity
or harbouring an urge to be dunked like a witch
it was bufoonery... tomfoolery...
a Deleuzian assault on the field of intensity
I like to grimace... I like to splutter...
I aspire to be picked out from the skies and hailed as a meteor
I was high on nearby fungi
I was dictating alexandrines about the climate into my phone
or did I seek... did I seek...
did I secretly think—*no! my public needs me!*
or—*how utterly divine to have the rug*
pulled out from under me—

SPRING DANCE

She hated all things girly, walked on walls,
chucked cores at boys, jeering, so when the season
turned all froufrou, turned all flouncy and the kerosene
of lawns laced the air, she stripped the garments

from her dolly (not a Barbie but of the genus Chunky
Peachie Plastic-Bodied Dolly) and pegged her scratchy
tresses to the line, and since the time was more than ripe,
she grabbed and lobbed tomatoes from their daddy's hothouse,

lobbed and lobbed and lobbed until they splattered
into scarlet pulpmash war wounds, worn, you might say,
proudly, by Mistress Dolly, who shimmied
midst the blossoms in the breeze.

MEDICAL NOTES
(i: history)

you could say I was old before my time soon after I was born
some of my limbs were cast in plaster igniting in me a lifelong
fascination with representations of the self—Early Onset
Posterity Complex you might baptize it if you were trying to
drum up a textbook definition—and soon after I was not even
walking or Tiny Tim-ing it around I was perched up on my
father's shoulder looking down at the world from a Parrot's
Eye View which seems to have affected my young psyche in
addition perhaps also because they often called me Polly for
the fact I never shut up to the extent that if I had no other
audience I would sing *La Traviata* to a stuffed dog and not the
opera just the title—*La Travia...La Travia...La Travia-ah-ta*
on and on then later I adopted an eye patch but only wore it
privately being too shy to understand my true piratical nature
until much later though I could have suspected myself from
the fact that I was always drawn to those who liked to travel
or who listed to one side or who lived haphazardly from hand
to mouth yet could if they so wished take you down in a trice
with a cutlass

SUCKER PUNCH

I'm not so sure about all this abstraction.
Lately things have got very Wittgensteinian.

A fat beige pillar came for me in a station.
And a small wall stood up the next evening
and punched me in the ribs. Damn near

broke them. I mean ok, I get it. It was night.
And you have to keep your wits (et cetera

et cetera) but this was a well-to-do wall
in a well-to-do area. I tell you it's not the blow
that winded me; more the betrayal.

APPLICATION FOR THE ROLE OF HERMIT

I see maps in the entrails of roadkill
I can fashion small meals from snails
my bloodline is the bloodline of bards
I creep about most days in a suit amongst
petty men—It's not me
I'm outdoorsy

I own a sheepskin pelt
I am prepared to primal dance
I want to go back to my roots
I want to eat roots

I am a man of few words
I am a man of no words
I can sleep in a tree
I have prehensile thumbs

I am calloused
I am bearded
I am a calloused, bearded, prehensile son of the soil
and of bards

I can turn my hand to poetry
I have by heart several fragments from antiquity
I can hang them from the trees
or carve them into bark
I can scrawl them in the gravel by the water feature

or I can zip it
totally

make like a high-end
sculpture out beyond the ha-ha
sitting in the Burmese posture

unblinking

or I can
blink

—I'm flexible

you choose

I thought about going to a support group. I looked into it in the Yellow Pages and other outmoded data sets. I came upon a strange group of surly Sues and churlish Chads. We sat around and made high-pitched whines for about an hour. It was a pre-verbal kind of vibe. Some of us barked. We were all royally pissed off by something or other but no one was allowed to say what. That was the beauty of it. In Week Two, we harmonised and made a lovely Whingey Symphony. A person from an Adult Ed course down the hall put their head round, looking for their dog, Brian Eno, who had strayed. We went full-scale *allegro con moans*. We premiered our *Suite for Gasps and Tuts and Clicks and Oufs and Sighs and Wails and Growls and Grrrs* and he staggered back in the collective blast of our exasperation that definitively proved neither Brian Eno the producer nor Brian Eno the Scottish terrier was anywhere in that room.

TO BE A DOG—

to gambol and to sometimes
lollop through the meadow,
head, a yo-yo, beech-green eyes.

To be a German Shepherd dog
sniffing *einfach, einfach so*
in between botanic explorations

or a Vizsla—chieftain of the hunting
arts, Hungarian and fed on chops, or
oh to be a spaniel, simply that and

snuffle pungent mushrooms and
listen in on lachrymose and ancient
earthworms keening at winter's end.

To be wise to it and thump the ground
and bark three times for spring!

SALVAGE

I have opened a window

the day has been wasted

my casement window

I have opened a window

a superfluity of roses

I have opened a window

freed from stupor

leaned out and am leaning

soft clumps

the black cloud

I have opened a window

but a small bird

nothing below

but wonderment and carnage

it will turn off

let it not be said

I have opened a window

lay the cool breeze on my cheek

yellow grass

bowing their rotting heads

a room to some degree

I have opened a window

shed and am shedding

they don't go quietly

trailing me all day

what is there to send out

with a sleepy eye

it will shriek

on the wing

half its brain

THE SUBSTITUTES

All my alternative mothers line up in the courtyard to pass me along.
One picks lint from my coat. The next disapproves of my shoes.
A Sicilian matron pinches my cheek, crying *O mia cucciola! Cucciola!*
(confusing as it's not my name). A woman in steel-rimmed spectacles
hands me *Das Kapital* and a language manual, *Deutsch Direkt*, which
I dump, coughing, as a twinset-and-pearls sprays me with clouds of
Chanel and I'm swivelling into a curlers-and-marigolds, who thrusts
a sink plunger into my hands, insisting *I'm not Mrs Mop* and so
on and so forth: the rock chick who wants us to do some lines; a harpist
mummified in chiffon, who needs me to turn the page; the exec (remote
in a headset) drumming instructions to Infinite Loop; a meditating
yogi, complete with gong; and finally, very far off, I see her—my mother
billowing in a nightie, her beautiful face looking huffy and strained.
Where have you been? she asks when I reach her. *You've been ages.*
I've been waiting. Where have you been?

CLASSIFICATION

and when she arrived in this
country and they asked

> *What was it like going to school*
> *on a camel?*

my aunt said

> *No idea*
> *We're Italian*

but my father spoke Arabic
and when somebody sneezed
taught us one person should say

> *The bison have sneezed*

another reply

> *And milk*
> *has grown cheaper*

without stipulating further
into which camp
he thought
we fell

> (milk-seller/
> bison/
> other...?)

not at all removed

which has another name

the one I'm talking about

the River *River*

or sometimes

or *Old Man A*

or Ur-River

it's the one beside which

and darlings ran amok

chasing each other

which is to say inside

haunches of ancient venison

elements of sertraline

but I digress

they do say

(though it doesn't)

which is the first cousin

to my town's river

but this one

's name is

i.e. *his* River

The River A

which makes it sound like the very first river

but it's not

tusky creatures used to ramble

in the wrong coats and hats

for the sake of love

this river you might find

(remnants laced lately with trace

and a tinge of fluoride)

because sometimes still

River Where the Wild Thyme Blows

or *O River!*

or

O Lush River!

though an intelligent machine

furnished with the bare bones

might term it

River With Wailing Willows

in a State of Quasi

-Apocalyptic Abandon

as in

this willow is losing it

this willow

is having a major depersonalization event

this willow

's hair is Peak Bad Hair

this willow

went to market and never came back

this willow

and this willow

and the next

are all totally hacked off

with the swans

royal fatheads

gone all funny

like cutting you ice-cold

dead with only a

talk-to-the-wing

glide-by

grade-A Queen-of-Sheba

bitchface

whereas the rest of us

what do we do?

not much

except

drip

UNRESOLVED

coconut crabs
ate Amelia Earhart

   that much is supposed

what they couldn't digest
was sent for analysis

   but got re-routed
   and lost in transit

sometime later Shiotsu
fashioned from found materials

   a set of avant-garde
   windchimes

placed them in his zone
of meditation and ease

   on mild days they
   shivered harmoniously

but when the wind
was up

   something percussive
   and insistent

took apart
the structures of his mind

like a rat-a-tat
of bullets

like the bones
demanded answers

but what to tell them?

—what note
to strike?

MEDICAL NOTES
(ii: reading)

I noticed a sub-heading on a sheet peeping out from the overstuffed folder bearing my name—peeped just enough for me to catch two words: Dangerous Fantasist. The audacity. I was already feeling rather papery and wished to gather myself and have it out with the medic clutching the file there and then but she looked even more scarecrowish than I was feeling. Two wrecks. It should have been companionable. Even if we were heading towards an iceberg—both of us—it would have been nice to feel it was the same iceberg. That we were, so to speak, navigational kin. We weren't kin. Not if she had written those two words about me in her delightfully wandering hand—a really aggressively cosmopolitan way she had with her curly 'g's and 's's that could only be described as—sexy. She had written her two words in her sexy script, no doubt with some kind of Mont Blanc pen her rich grandfather had bestowed on her as a token of his delight at her entering the medical profession and now—here she was keeping catty notes about me whilst clearly on the cusp of losing it entirely for I could sense her breath coming in rasps, getting raggedier as she applied anaesthetic drops and attempted to manoeuvre the tonometer onto my eye so she could take an accurate pressure reading. Then she did a textbook SHARP INTAKE. Is it high—I said. She said—No! As if my question was presumptuous. As if she could quash me and my qualms outright but really who was I to believe a single word from her mouth after she had written me off so comprehensively with her note then coolly slipped it into my records and was even now wafting it right beneath my nose as if to take me for an absolute loon.

Capsized duck. Auto duck. Cut-throat duck. Long-nosed duck. Renaissance duck. Hench duck. Mensch duck. Full-throttle duck. Standardized duck. Truculent duck. Natty duck. Fatty duck. Fin de siècle duck. Hi-de-Hi duck. Cosmic duck. Tragic duck. Botox duck. Fluffy duck. Lardy duck. Mardy duck. Mucky duck. Remote duck. Kyoto duck. Live-in duck. Vermouth duck. Foolproof duck. Intermittent feedback duck. Canal duck. Halal duck. Catch-me-if-you-can duck. Lunar duck. Consumer duck. Do-as-you-would-be-done-to duck. Lucid duck. Macro duck. Panoramic view duck. Morose duck. Verbose duck. In-and-of-itself duck. Crinklecut duck. Smash-and-grab duck. On-you-go duck. Walk-the-plank duck. Down-amongst-the-dead-ducks duck. Where would we be without you, duck?

MAY DAY IN MARBELLA

Chronology's scrambled! scream the swifts
when we get there and we keep on missing you

as the birds make their ragged ascensions
shrieking *Stick it chronology!* and below, the sea

catching its breath, catching it over and over
as you did all that day, until you stopped. Time

slipped and the sea oh my God, going for an Oscar
with its splashy theatrics, its Pinteresque pauses—

how it dries and forgets its line, but always
comes back, which stings, because you can't.

You're not here now—but also here you are
behind a pillar savouring the Turkish concerto

in the Iglesia de la Encarnación and in the gardens
beside Dali's giant (the shadow isn't Don Quixote's

it's yours). And when we find a tooth-shaped stone
on the shore (bright molar of the Mediterranean)

it's your voice I hear laugh *What maw do you think
coughed it up?*—before you dip backwards, into the blue.

AGITATIONS (IN THAT YEAR INCLUDED)

Fear of Death by Plague, Fear of Death by Serial Killer Hiding Out on Nearby Common, Fear of Death by Large Dog, Fear of Death by Mutated Form of Virus Occasioned by Living Near Squirrels, Fear of Death from Eyestrain, Fear of Death from Hand Sanitizer-Related Eczema, Fear of Death from Intense Fixation on Death, Fear of Death from Shopping Trolleys, Fear of Death from Redundant Satellite Falling on Head, Fear of Death from Inertia, Fear of Death from Insufficient Breathing, Fear of Death by Slipping through the Portal between Then and Now, Fear of Death from Crying Jags, Fear of Death from Pillows, Fear of Death from Increased Lifespan of the Wasp, Fear of Death from Over-Gargling with Salt, Fear of Death from Teeth Falling Out and Being Unable to Chew Solids, Fear of Death from Air Quality, Fear of Death by Fashion Suicide, Fear of Death from Washcloths, Fear of Death from Rare Mould, Fear of Death by Non-Stop Chirrup of Failing Batteries in Neighbour's Garage, Fear of Death from Tick, Fear of Death from Choking on Supersized Vitamin D, Fear of Death from Discovery in the Mirror of Miss Havisham, Fear of Death by Spontaneous Combustion, Fear of Death from Use of Past-Expiry-Date Aromatic Room Diffuser, Fear of Death from Ennui, Fear of Death from Weltschmerz, Fear of Death from Unstoppable Outpouring of Untranslatable Woe, Fear of Death by Co-op Robot, by Tuk-Tuk, by Body Clocks De-Syncing, by Slow Sinking Feeling, by Close Encounter with Own Overgrown Hair.

AFTERMATH

If you were here we might discuss it all

                        the rhyme schemes of starlings
                        the ramifications of squirrels
                        that creature, that hyena laughing
                        in the trees and how the blue hour
                        really feels and why it is that song
                        thrush always likes to smash
                        an escargot into the wall

LIBERATION

Do some frog-leaps every day and if that doesn't work, jump
sideways, left or right, like a crouching monkey.

Afternoons are optimal. The blood is sluggish in the veins
after two, and something lumpen in the stomach causes torpor.

Push past it. Invite Vitality and her sister Spontaneity must follow.
Try camel-struts or walk on your hands like a red Himalayan bear,

or squat and waddle like a duck—any duck, even an aged,
arthritic duck, martyr to some duckish malady. Or pad or slither or

trot. Why not trot? Adopt the semi-feral trot of a let's say Konic not
Shetland pony, wind-whipped, dead set on ditching her hareem.

Dear Mistress Ocularist: Thank you for your services but I respectfully point out you have made me look boss-eyed, nay cock-eyed, nay oddly agog. You have given me a far-off skew-whiff glint. You have made me unnervingly awry. I look askance at everything. I look askance at breakfast, lunch and tea. I wear the face of the reject doll that the doll factory has donated to an underfunded charity. I wear the face of the possessed doll that plays a pivotal role in a scene of paranormal activity in a nineteen-seventies classic slasher movie. Walking along, among nature, my rapt expression startles local animals. I appear to be scowling through my nose at all times in all directions. I seem more than usually brusque and in a state of almost perpetual alarum. In short, madam, I expected harmony and find myself sadly unable to strike anything other, with this bum eye, than a bum note. So that's what I wrote.

was massy and abundant and Michel professed it acted
as a barrier against contagion, citing the fact he never
once caught plague as proof indisputable of its sublime
proficiency as microbe-barricade par excellence.

I think I'll grow one

dense and luxuriant, a display that will erase all
question marks regarding the extent of my personal
virility and I will oil it. Oh I will oil its splendour into
two twin tapering spikes that at moments of high
stress I shall, with abandon, twirl artistically.

Let's face it—it will come in handy.

NOT EVERYTHING HAS TO BE A SONNET

Take this moment beside the rapids,
where sunlight clips the old weir wall,
knowing itself to be only a faint replica
of sunlight, not the sort found in other
places, like Pisa or Nairobi, but without
undue dismay at its shortcomings and
invisibly corpsing, here and there, as
only the old-style comics knew how,
with little, hiccupy giggles incorporated
seamlessly into their acts, which
is what this bit of sun does out of glee,
perhaps, or relief to find itself watery
—yes, ravaged—sure, but hitting the
black waters soundly and giddy with it.
Going nowhere fast.

HIERARCHY

the Blue Drawing Room
is above the Abbot's
Sitting Room

the blue fireplace is
above the
Abbot's fireplace

(below that—
fireplaces
all the way down)

the East Wing
—missing
in action

the deer
in the deer park
—eaten

antlers over
the Great
Door

a woman under
-neath wheezing
in chiffon

dear lady

(up since dawn
roping
things off)

do you know
can you say the
real reason

why
the fish
sank?

the mistress
fled?
what the King

was doing for
so many
days—

half-in/
half-out of that
window?

I take exception to a life skills class
where the skills are non-applicable and go
out to stand on the brow of a hill beneath the dome
of a one-of-a-kind windmill, attributed by some to Inigo Jones,
by others to a Jonesian disciple. I stand strong like a brute, like I've hoisted
the millstone right up to the grinding loft myself. Blissful. I could crow.
What to tell you? These gifts are given.

NOTICE TO GUESTS:

'If we find abandoned deckchairs with towels on them, we will bring the towels to reception'

We will do this to advance the cause of justice.
We will do this because pleasure must be paid.
We will do this to combat non-commodious feng shui.
We will do this because most men love beauty more than they love virtue.
We will do this to atone for other errors of judgement.
We will do this so as not to tip entirely over the edge.
We will threaten to do this but we may or may not come through.
We will do this according to no strict rota.
We will do this to keep you on your toes.
We will drill novice attendants in noiselessness and stealth.
We will be sudden.
We will be swift.
Afterwards you will ask yourselves: How? Why?
We will do this for your own good not ours.

VIOLETTOMANIA

I got my diagnosis last year after I went away on holiday.
I would spend hours staring out of the dining-room window.
All I could see was mauve, indigo, *blu dipinto di blu*

and yes, I admit, it was awkward. People couldn't get past me
to access the continental breakfast, it was a sort of social
death, really, no one would choose the sun lounger

next to mine but I was ok. I had my bluegrass mashup of
'Volare' and 'Purple Rain' to work on, so there I'd sit
strumming my midnight-blue ukulele—*Hang on to your soul!*

I'd holler at an inside-out pool umbrella or storm-tossed
palm or for the benefit of the gulls battered sideways (*Hang on
to your souls!*) into UV and burnt-out stars.

MARTYRS

Sometimes we give them a hard time, the martyrs.
Look at you—we shout—*with your tragic backstory
and your little legs and your incompetent veins.*

Want me to knit you a hair-shirt? Sometimes we
shout that too (even though you can't knit hair). Or
we go *Dudda Da Duuuh* like we're Beethoven's

Fifth Symphony kicking in. The martyrs meanwhile
don't abate. They are dancing across the kingdoms
of this world and the next. They are relentless

terpsichoreans. Even their sneezes sound like Ravel's
Bolero. Even the candlewax dropped on their smocks
makes ornamental masterpieces of their sleeves.

THE LEFTOVERS

Most of us these days are dead or on autopilot.
As for the wolves—they thrive.
There are too many wolves—some complain bitterly.
They pad into the butchers.
They make off with small inflatables and sail about
like Vikings licking their bloody chops.
Others can't get enough of their uptick
—their soundless transition from wilderness spook
to denizen of the high street where they glide up and
down, up and down or bask in the rubble
while the acolytes forage like mad
for something to offer them—Kentucky
Fried Chicken. Small birds.

THE DEATH OF POETRY

was drawn-out
but fun

there was a bonfire
with those
small sausages
on sticks

we all whooped
it up on
homebrew

afterwards
—not much

some-
body's dead
uncle with a space
for a face
onto which we projected
our various longings
and fears
hung about for a time—

a clutch
of haiku (bad)
came of that

and one
stab (thank God,
only one)
at an elegy

then nothing

—for a bit

then
a wren
blew in
who an expert
swore
had sung
an entire saga
in the original
Norse

(they ran tests
but it died)

finally bull
-dozers brought
down the whole
place for
flats with a top-
notch gym
on the
side

some bright
spark
branded it *Poetry
in Motion*

—we really
really did laugh

shuffling across the carpark from the pool in my dry robe
like a damp, disconsolate Cistercian, I heard them,
two peacocks: their proclamations launched wide into the
whites of the Cumbrian sky, their maladroit plainsong cutting
up the backdrop of chaffinch after chaffinch and as if from
nowhere, two peacocks: (stately home dropouts? heritage
park rejects?) with a message from beyond or with no
message but voluble on matters unfathomable and in the
darkness of my cabin with my shut-up grief and neural
scramble, what a boon to hear the boundlessness of those
two peacocks: broadcasting in peacock across the night

GLORIA

You who are splendidly acted (though the yawns seem a trifle put on) hiccup beside the rockpools in this era of confinement.

A thin whippety wind. A new kind of awake they call asleep. The children yell their concatenations, cut knees, hunt

crabs, fight, kill, et cetera. Everyone is out today. Loving and murdering. Skirting the lardy oil drums. I give thanks for every

scrap. Cut-glass rain. Yafflers. Your very charitable ear.

and where yesterday I lay broiling in the vat of my bedroom
today a sneaky little breeze tickles my soles—*Coo-ee! Only me!*
shifty at first but soon breeze picks up speed with *What—*
did you think I was gone for good? That me and my three 'e's had
danced our final conga around your curtains and hightailed it
out of the element once and for all? Finita la commedia?
Leaving you with only the hot, hot heat to tan your hide?
My God, you're a tragedian. I bet you spent the whole 48-hour
heatwave being Blanche Dubois around the place, fainting
and drawing cold baths. Don't tell me. I bet you were writing poetry.
Oh God, you were. Oh you have to have your psychodrama, don't you?
You can't resist. Come on—give me a couplet you've come up with,
something nice and plangent, and I'll write it across the skies.
You'd like that, wouldn't you? Admit it. Speak up. But I didn't speak.
I didn't dare interrupt. It was so good to have breeze back and babbling
on—ruffling my feathers as he always used to, as if he always would,
as if nothing in the world was any different from the way it had been before.

BEFORE THERE WERE WORDS—

words like *acrimony* and *amertume*
before somebody came along
trying to cram the hard graininess
of disagreement into language
before all that, there were birds

some really quite big ones
a rude person might say *elephantine*
which would be harsh because the thing is
they still flew, that's the miracle of it
however wide of girth and unwieldy
they were with their big, blocky heads
these massive prehistoric lumberers

sailed upwards and coasted around
on the westerlies and northerlies
of ancient time—they didn't feel
gauche or non-svelte, they felt beautiful
all airy and agenda-less, quite caught
up in their meandering (sometimes
bellowed) improvisations across vast
expanses, and serene—happy
even in the knowledge they could
be purple, if the mood took them
but also, any time they liked
they could be mauve.

ACCOMPANIMENT

Stood for ages waiting for the sun to turn up and pay
homage to a clutch of brilliant orange poppies.

It declined. But the poppies couldn't be bothered to get
hung up on feelings of betrayal and bobbed about—

ditsy and undimmed—perhaps slightly drunk on some
fringe classic I couldn't catch beneath the growl

of road construction. Sonata for a cabbage white, solo-
fluttered? Maybe a soft-shoe shuffle from the ants?

it is 2.59 pm four days after Bastille Day and a heatwave and I am longing to see *A Bundle of Asparagus* by Adrian S. Coorte at the Fitzwilliam Museum Cambridge but there are obstacles such as for a start there are too many blocks of cement between me and the asparagus so I will have to forgo the pleasure even though it would be beyond words nice just now to see the dark woody tones and be reminded of damp earth and fecundity in a simple not quite renaissance kind of way and my mind instead of lumbering around inside its skull-case like a half-baked hippopotamus would be becalmed would have found in essence its mudhole if it could sit and wallow in the asparagus and recognise that such things as freshness and verdure do exist and have not been scorched into annihilation at every turn but it would require as I say too much back-breaking sun bouncing off concrete to get there and anyway as it's a Monday the museum is shut so I'd have to break in and the streets being extra still I would show up easily on a policeman's radar even accepting the fact that some of those policemen might have bunked off and be even now swimming along Snob's Stream or one of the other minor tributaries of the river Cam not wanting to be caught in a hotspot, not wanting to add to the already inflamed sense of outrage at how the peacekeepers and guardians and father figures of our time are sorely lacking and even if I didn't break in and I could slip in through an old stone archway and a wooden door that's been left ajar Cambridge being full of such portals even if I could step over the latticework of criss-crossing laser beams intended to prevent someone shoving *A Bundle of Asparagus* under one arm and making off with it even if I could choreograph it right so as to slide into a cool dim alcove and sit to meditate in total solitude on the asparagus maybe I wouldn't be alone maybe I'd meet a stray old lady bussed in from a hamlet in Hampshire who went to the loo at an inopportune moment and never saw her coach party again and has been wandering around the museum throughout all of Sunday night and who got so hungry she wanted to eat the asparagus and who got so desperate she lay down for a time in imitation of Nicholas Poussin's *Extreme Unction* (1638-1640) but then stood up again because really pretending to be a corpse doesn't help anyone especially if you're in a museum especially at night on your own and if we do meet (she half-crazed but with a last stick of liquorice in her handbag) maybe we'll sit together counting the pale green spears on the very dark background contemplating how something so luscious can be an optical illusion and if flowers mean tempus fugit what the hell does asparagus mean

life	what are you doing
life	all got up like that
life	an essay crisis
life	lost the crib sheet
life	nouns and verbs
life	what's this for
life	uniform options
life	these those that their thou
life	my molars hurt
life	more nouns and verbs
life	do I know you
life	my late friend
life	in the cupboard
life	doubtless you'll have heard
life	collapsible lungs
life	wearing well
life	beetroot and horseradish
life	took it to the grave
life	don't run
life	in the corridor
life	and by corridor
life	I mean everywhere
life	fits and starts
life	I think you'll find
life	something bit her
life	near the Achilles
life	made a boo-boo
life	brave girl
life	pioneering treatment
life	rise at dawn
life	swear by dauphinoise

life   a cut above mash
life   contra-indications
life   listed in brief
life   direct enquiries
life   to the voluptuary
life   rouge et noir
life   looks good on you
life   overweening rogue
life   masculine ending
life   Death Valley
life   without the snacks
life   on a slow day
life   regular bouts
life   low moan
life   pick yourself up
life   an act of contrition
life   the carotid
life   resistance really
life   is the wet look
life   do you know anything about
life   muffled drums
life   the whole world
life   it's a franchise
life   goes on a bit
life   there now
life   wasn't so bad
life   was it
life   I prefer the spin-off
life   Porlock
life   who he
life   just my little
life

REMEMBER THE FLAMINGO

pushing the white pipe
-cleaner of her neck
around the waters
of the lagoon

such a bright day

the pale juvenile
beneath the surface
looked up hope
-fully

and did the same

ACKNOWLEDGEMENTS

Grateful acknowledgements are due to the editors of the following publications, in which versions of some of these poems first appeared: *The Poetry Review*, *The New Statesman*, *The Idler*, *Poetry Ireland Review*, *Granta*, *The Rialto*, *PN Review*, *The Spectator*, *The Tangerine*, *Bad Lilies*, *The North*, *Times Literary Supplement.*

'The Substitutes' was first published in *The Book of Bad Betties* (Bad Betty Press, 2021).

Thank you to my family and friends for their love, inspiration and patient listening, and to the many who have helped with brilliant advice along the way, especially Danielle, Becca, Tara, Emma, Penny, Jo, David, Liz, and all the pandemic crew – Kate, Ben, Ian, Paul and Adam – for invaluable Zoom chats. Huge thanks to Greta Stoddart and Michael Symmons Roberts for their generous support and to John McAuliffe, Michael Schmidt, Andrew Latimer, Nelson Mackay, Jazmine Linklater and all at Carcanet.